TOP

HIGH SCHOOL SPORTS

CHEERLEADING

A Crabtree Branches Book

THOMAS KINGSLEY TROUPE

CRABTREE
Publishing Company
www.crabtreebooks.com

School-to-Home Support for Caregivers and Teachers

This high-interest book is designed to motivate striving students with engaging topics while building fluency, vocabulary, and an interest in reading. Here are a few questions and activities to help the reader build upon his or her comprehension skills.

Before Reading:

- *What do I think this book is about?*
- *What do I know about this topic?*
- *What do I want to learn about this topic?*
- *Why am I reading this book?*

During Reading:

- *I wonder why...*
- *I'm curious to know...*
- *How is this like something I already know?*
- *What have I learned so far?*

After Reading:

- *What was the author trying to teach me?*
- *What are some details?*
- *How did the photographs and captions help me understand more?*
- *Read the book again and look for the vocabulary words.*
- *What questions do I still have?*

Extension Activities:

- *What was your favorite part of the book? Write a paragraph on it.*
- *Draw a picture of your favorite thing you learned from the book.*

TABLE OF CONTENTS

GIVE ME A V!

The crowd groans as the home team loses a big play on the field. You and your cheerleading squad know what to do. The music blares as you and your teammates dance and get the fans in the stands chanting. In no time, the crowd is on their feet, cheering their team to victory!

4

Grab your pom-poms and megaphone! We're about to learn why cheerleading ranks among the... TOP HIGH SCHOOL SPORTS.

FUN FACT

Cheerleading is considered one of the most dangerous sports for girls. Injuries include broken bones, concussions, and torn ligaments, like the ACL.

CHEERLEADING HISTORY

Cheerleading started in Great Britain during in the 1860s. In the 1880s, cheerleading reached the United States. Thomas Peebles introduced the idea of chanting to **spectators** at the University of Minnesota. There, Johnny Campbell led the first organized cheer during a game against Princeton University in 1898.

At the time, cheerleading was a male-dominated sport. It wasn't until the 1920s that women became involved in cheerleading.

A CHEER FROM PRINCETON (1884):

Ray, Ray, Ray!
Tiger, Tiger, Tiger!
Sis, Sis, Sis!
Boom, Boom, Boom
Aaaaah! Princeton, Princeton, Princeton!

Four United States Presidents were cheerleaders years before their big job at the White House. They included Franklin D. Roosevelt from Harvard College, Dwight D. Eisenhower at West Point, Ronald Reagan for Eureka College, and George W. Bush while he attended Phillips Academy. Hooray for America!

WHY CHEERLEADING?

Cheerleading is an important part of high school sports. Cheerleaders not only encourage school spirit, but use their **enthusiasm** and energy to bring the team and the crowd together.

FUN FACT

The record for the largest team cheer was 2,102 cheerleaders in Hangzhou, Zhejiang, China. It featured people who were as young as 5 years old and as old as 68. The event was big enough to end up in the Guinness Book of World Records!

A good cheerleading squad uses music, dance, and athleticism to **energize** and entertain the crowd. Some would argue that they get as much exercise as the players they cheer for!

TRYOUTS

Like many high school sports, cheerleaders compete to make the team. Every high school is different, but for many the **tryout** process lasts an entire week. Participants will learn a cheer and dance each day.

On the day of tryouts, there are usually three to five judges who will score on categories such as spirit, ability, and eye contact.

FUN FACT

There are around 3.5 million cheerleaders in the United States alone.

VARSITY AND JUNIOR VARSITY TEAMS

High school cheerleading squads are often divided by sport and by classes. The JV (Junior Varsity) squads are usually made up of first- and second-year students. This squad is where cheerleaders will learn the basics while cheering for JV teams.

Junior Varsity

The varsity level squads are mostly third- or fourth-year cheerleaders. Varsity cheerleaders can often do more advanced dance moves and **gymnastics** as they cheer for the varsity level teams.

Varsity

Cheerleaders were historically seen at high school football or basketball games, but that has changed over the years. Some cheerleading squads make appearances at baseball, soccer, volleyball, and wrestling matches. Every sports crowd could use some help cheering!

13

ROLES IN CHEERLEADING

There are three basic roles in most cheerleading squads. They are:

Flyer — The cheerleader lifted up or tossed into the air is a flyer. They end up as the center of attention. It might look easy, but a flyer's role is physically **demanding**...and dangerous.

Bases — The foundation of any stunt that launches or lifts the flyer into the air is a base. They are usually taller and stronger and use good technique to keep themselves and flyers from getting hurt.

Spotter — Similar to a base, spotters are used to help steady or balance cheerleading stunts. They are also the first point of contact when a flyer **dismounts** or falls.

FLYER

SPOTTER

BASE

EQUIPMENT & UNIFORMS

Cheerleaders will often use pom-poms, usually in the school's colors, to attract attention. Many use megaphones to boost the volume of their voice.

megaphone

Most cheerleading squads wear uniforms displaying their school colors and mascot. Girls typically wear skirts and boys usually wear athletic pants. Both wear similar sleeveless shirts. In colder weather, warmer pants and sweaters are worn.

FUN FACT

The word pom-pom comes from the French word *pompe*, which means tuft of ribbons.

CHEERS, CHANTING, AND PEP RALLIES

One of the biggest goals for a cheerleading squad is to boost the crowd's energy. Many cheers and chants are about team pride and school spirit.

Some high schools hold pep rallies. These are school gatherings to generate excitement before a big game. Often cheerleaders will lead these rallies to cheer and perform dance routines. The school band will play music to get the crowd going.

DANCING AND STUNTING

Most times, cheerleading is about entertaining the spectators at the game. To do this, some cheerleading squads play music and perform a dance routine to pump up the crowd.

Some more advanced cheerleading teams might perform what is called stunting. This can include lifting cheerleaders into the air, doing gymnastics, or forming a human **pyramid** with the entire crew.

PRACTICE AND CHEERLEADING CAMPS

Like any high-impact sport, cheerleading takes lots of practice. Most squads will practice stunting and dances after school. They want to make sure they're ready to perform in front of the crowd.

Many places offer cheerleading camps where cheerleaders can stay to improve their skills. Campers will form closer team bonds and work on **tumbling**, dance moves, and team stunts.

The National Cheerleading Association (NCA) was founded in 1948 by former cheerleader Lawrence Herkimer. He believed cheerleaders could perform better if they trained outside the school year. He started the first cheer training camp the very next year in 1949.

FRIDAY NIGHT GAMES

Cheerleaders are an important part of high school football games. Most schools have their games on Friday night under the bright lights on a crisp, autumn evening.

During these popular games, cheerleaders often tailor their cheers to what's happening in the game. The noise from the stands and the sidelines reminds the players on the field that everyone is counting on them to bring home the win!

CHEERLEADING COMPETITIONS

The athletes cheerleaders support aren't the only ones who get to compete! Cheerleading has become such a **competitive** sport that there's a national championship held every year.

FUN FACT

The most recent NHSCC competition featured 950 teams! Squads from 34 states in the United States and 9 countries competed in the 2020 competition.

The National High School Cheerleading Championship (NHSCC) happens annually in Orlando, Florida. The best high school cheerleading squads from around the country and world compete to see who is number one!

CONCLUSION

Cheerleading is one of the most action-packed sports high-schoolers participate in. It takes skill, energy, and school spirit to come out on top. Games really wouldn't be the same without cheerleaders.

Will you practice your backflips and perform in front of the crowd? Maybe you and your squad will go to the nationals. With practice and dedication, you'll see why cheerleading is definitely one of the TOP HIGH SCHOOL SPORTS!

GLOSSARY

ACL (AY-SEE-EL): an abbreviation for anterior cruciate ligament, a body part that stabilizes the knee joint

competitive (kuhm-PET-uh-tiv): attempting to be as good or better than others

demanding (di-MAN-ding): a task requiring skill and effort

dismounts (diss-MOUNTS): finishing moves of students or gymnastics tricks

energize (EN-ur-jize): to supply energy to something

enthusiasm (en-THOO-zee-az-uhm): intense excitement

gymnastics (jim-NASS-tiks): a sport that displays physical agility and coordination

pyramid (PIHR-uh-mid): a triangular shape with a large base and a pointy top

spectators (SPEK-tay-turz): people in a crowd gathered to watch

tryout (TRY-out): to test the potential of a person or thing

tumbling (TUM-bul-ing): performing acrobatic or gymnastic exercises

INDEX

WEBSITES TO VISIT

https://kids.kiddle.co/Cheerleader

https://www.dkfindout.com/us/sports/gymnastics/

https://kids.britannica.com/students/article/
cheerleading/319406

31

ABOUT THE AUTHOR

Thomas Kingsley Troupe

Thomas Kingsley Troupe is the author of a big ol' pile of books for kids. He's written about everything from ghosts to Bigfoot to third grade werewolves. He even wrote a book about dirt. When he's not writing or reading, he gets plenty of exercise and remembers sacking quarterbacks while on his high school football team. Thomas lives in Woodbury, Minnesota with his two sons.

CRABTREE
Publishing Company

Written by: Thomas Kingsley Troupe
Designed by: Jennifer Dudyk
Edited by: Kelli Hicks
Proofreader: Ellen Rodger

Photographs: Cover background pattern (and pattern throughout book © HNK/Shutterstock.com, pom pom on cover and title page © Dana Zurkiyeh/Shutterstock.com, cover photo of cheerleaders © Thomas Carter | Dreamstime.com. Following images from Shutterstock.com: Page 4 top photo © Rob Byron, bottom photo © Poznyakov, Page 5 © View Apart, Page 6 © chippix, Page 9 top photo © nullplus, bottom photo © Aleksei Lazukov, Page 10 © Pressmaster, Page 12 bottom photo © Joseph Sohm, Page 13 and Page 15 (spotter) © WoodysPhotos, Page 15 (base) © Cherednychenko Ihor, Page 16 bottom photo © WoodysPhotos, Page 17 © LightField Studios, Page 18 © Joseph Sohm, Page 19 bottom photo © JoeSAPhotos, Page 23 top photo © Richard Thornton, bottom photo © TommyStockProject, Page 25 top photo © Joseph Sohm, Page 27 bottom photo © Pavel L Photo and Video, Page 29 bottom photo © nullplus. Following images from istock by Getty Images: Pages 8, 11, top photo Page 19, bottom photo Page 25, top photos Pages 27 and 29 © Roberto Galan, Page 12 top photo © Joseph Calomeni, Page 22 © marieclaudelemay, Following images from Dreamstime.com: Page 15 (flyer) Pavel Losevsky, Page 16 top photo © Sports Images, Page 19 bottom photo © Molly Williams, Page 20 © Aspenphoto, Page 21 top photo © Joe Sohm, bottom photo Thomas Carter, Page 24 © Joe Sohm, Page 26 © Ritmoboxer, Page 28 © Reinout Van Wagtendonk. Page 7 photo courtesy of the Library of Congress

Library and Archives Canada
Cataloguing in Publication

CIP available at Library and
Archives Canada

Library of Congress Cataloging-in-Publication Data

CIP available at Library of Congress

Crabtree Publishing Company

www.crabtreebooks.com   1-800-387-7650

Printed in the U.S.A./CG20210915/012022

Published in the United States
Crabtree Publishing
347 Fifth Avenue, Suite 1402-145
New York, NY, 10016

Published in Canada
Crabtree Publishing
616 Welland Ave.
St. Catharines, Ontario L2M 5V6